Joy and the Monster

Zandria Solomon

By Zandria Solomon

Illustrations: Dorothy Roland

ISBN: 9781729343685

DEDICATION

To a safer future for our children.

CONTENTS

ACKNOWLEDGMENT

To my on Earth guardian angel: Thank you for everything! Thank you for all the love and support you have given me when I had no one else. I don't know how I could ever repay you,; but here's a start:

this book is dedicated to the one and only: Faith Saunders.

Dear Reader,

It is with great pride that I introduce my new book "Joy and the Monster."
First off, I would like to thank everyone who has been supporting and encouraging me to pursue my dream as a writer. Despite the challenges, the journey was fulfilling.
I am very proud of this book and the subject matter it presents. I understand it may not be a topic most people like to talk about. This is the first of a series of books about Joy and her family as they conquer real life issues most people face on a daily basis but who also find it difficult to talk about.

My objective in writing these books is to create a safe environment for all children by giving them the tools they need to protect themselves against some of life's real dangers. As a child, I thought the only monsters to worry about were vampires, aliens, the big green monster under the bed, or possessed dolls I watched on television. However, once I turned seven, a family friend abused me sexually. This person became a "monster" in my eyes; one that I felt powerless against because I did not know how to protect myself or seek help. It is devastating to realize real people can become "monsters", and unfortunately it is sometimes people who are very close to us. I believe the best way to protect our loved ones is to have these conversations. I hope my books will give parents and their children the opportunity to talk openly about these difficult topics in a more comfortable way.

I wholeheartedly believe sharing my experience will help a child and his/her family some day. Now that I am a mother myself, I understand how necessary it is to talk about these difficult topics and I am now more passionate about creating this series of books.

To all the victims who are still struggling through this terrible pain, I need you to know that I understand. You are not alone and you can beat this. To all the survivors who overcame and rose above the pain, keep your heads up and push forward.

Thank you,
Zandria Solomon.

Joy
and the
Monster

When Joy was four years old, she watched "Monsters Under My Bed" with her best friend Ziggy.

Since then, she has had trouble sleeping alone.

Joy just turned 7 years old but she is still scared of the Monster that lives under her bed. She has become too scared to sleep alone now.

Her mom thinks she is overreacting, but her dad loves comforting his little princess whenever she is scared.

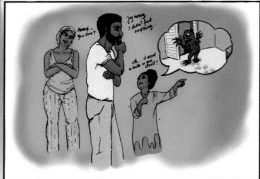

Her mom thinks it is time for her to be a big girl and start sleeping alone again.

But, Joy is nervous and believes the Monster still lives under her bed.

So, to make it easier for Joy, her mom bought her a night light and a teddy bear.

Joy's mom comforted her and told her that her dad can protect her from any monster.

They agreed that her dad would be on "Monster Inspection" duty every night.

For the first time in a long time, Joy felt so much better and began sleeping in her own room again!

Over the next few nights, Joy slept soundly.
She even turned off the night light by day five.

Since she had been sleeping like a big girl,
her dad told her he had a big surprise
for her after school.

Joy was so excited she could not stop
staring at her school's clock all day long.

She could not wait to see the
surprise waiting for her.

As soon as school ended, Joy rushed outside. She could not believe who came to pick her up!

It was her favorite uncle Oscar!!

Uncle Oscar was always offering to help take care of Joy so that her parents could take a night out.

One Friday, he told her that they were going to have a special movie night with all her favorite snacks.

At some point during the movie, Joy got really scared. Her uncle said he would protect her and then sat her down on his lap.

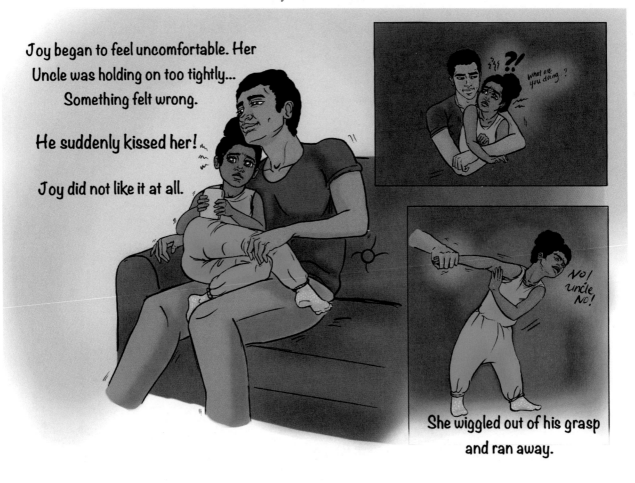

The next morning, Joy ran to the kitchen to tell her dad what happened. She was feeling very bad.

She was hoping he would be alone. But, when she got there, she was surprised to see uncle Oscar already sitting at the kitchen table. She froze!

Her dad noticed and asked her what was wrong. She shrugged and said she forgot to brush her teeth.

Joy pretended she was sick so she could spend the whole weekend in her room to avoid uncle Oscar. Her parents ended up believing that she was ill.

Her mom brought her chicken soup and crackers so she could feel better.

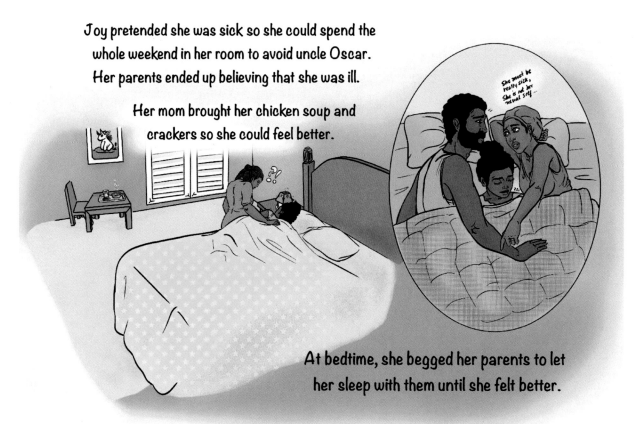

At bedtime, she begged her parents to let her sleep with them until she felt better.

On Monday, Joy said she felt better and
wanted to go to school. Her mom was relieved to see that Joy
was ready to leave her room. Joy's mom helped her
get ready and then walked her to the bus.

As soon as Joy got on the bus and saw her best friend Ziggy, she broke down and cried. She then explained to Ziggy what happened.

Then, Ziggy told her that her parents said if anyone does a bad thing to children, they should not be scared to tell their mom and dad.

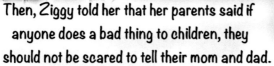

When they got to the school, Ziggy told Joy they needed to tell Mrs Thompson, the Principal, everything.

She led Joy by the hands to Mrs Thompson's office and explained to her what happened to her best friend.

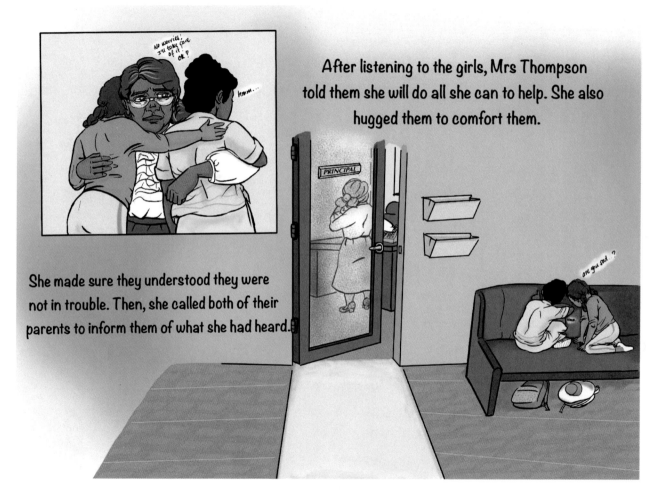

After listening to the girls, Mrs Thompson told them she will do all she can to help. She also hugged them to comfort them.

She made sure they understood they were not in trouble. Then, she called both of their parents to inform them of what she had heard.

When the parents got to the school, they became very upset about what they heard, especially Joy's parents.

They knew they needed to send the "Monster" away.

The parents were very proud of their girls for being so brave. Joy's parents could not wait to give their little girl her biggest hug ever.

Joy's parents comforted their little girl and
told her how much they love her, and how they
will always be there to help her. They also
reassured her that uncle Oscar would never hurt her again.

THE END.

Activity section: Let's Talk!

Note to parents: use the following questions as a guideline to have a comprehensive conversation with your child.

1. What did you think of the Story?

2. Who was the "monster" in the book?

3. Why did Joy began to feel uncomfortable with Uncle Oscar?
   (Segway to discuss intuition).

4. Why did Joy tell her best friend Ziggy instead of her mom what happened to her?

5. Who else are you comfortable telling if something happens to you?
   (Segway to reassuring the child that they can come to you for anything.)

Joy loves small animals.

Joy loves taking silly pictures with Ziggy.

Joy loves spending time with her parents.

END OF ACTIVITY SECTION.

NOTE FROM THE AUTHOR

I am a survivor of child abuse and now a mother of two beautiful little girls. In writing this book, I hope to facilitate discussions on difficult subjects within families; in doing so, I wish it could give young children and adolescents the necessary tools to face life's many different monsters.

THANK YOU FOR READING.

Made in the USA
Columbia, SC
22 July 2021